What Is
God's Will
for My Life?

Richard A. Jensen

What Is God's Will for My Life?

Ten Questions Christians Most Often Ask

AUGSBURG Publishing House • Minneapolis

WHAT IS GOD'S WILL FOR MY LIFE?
Ten Questions Christians Most Often Ask

Copyright © 1988 Augsburg Publishing House

Library of Congress Cataloging-in-Publication Data

Jensen, Richard A.
  WHAT IS GOD'S WILL FOR MY LIFE?

  1. Lutheran Church—Sermons. 2. God—Will—Sermons.
3. Sermons, American. I. Title.
BX8066.J46W48   1988   252'.041   88-22295
ISBN 0-8066-2365-9

Manufactured in the U.S.A.   APH 10-7048

    2   3   4   5   6   7   8   9   0   1   2   3   4   5   6   7   8   9

About the Author

What Is God's Will for My Life? is the seventh collection of Richard Jensen's messages to have been published since he became speaker/director of Lutheran Vespers in June 1982. Dr. Jensen completed five books for a series on the gospel of Matthew: *Emmanuel; Hear These Words; Jesus Creates New Life; Jesus, Friend of Sinners;* and *Jesus Is Coming.* In 1985, eight of Dr. Jensen's messages dealing with the Holy Spirit were compiled into a book entitled, *Come, Holy Spirit.* He is also the author of two other books, both published by Augsburg Publishing House: *Touched by the Spirit* and *Telling the Story.*

Richard A. Jensen is an alumnus of Dana College and Trinity Seminary. He received his S.T.M. from the Lutheran School of Theology in Chicago and his Ph.D. from Aquinas Institute of Theology in Dubuque, Iowa. He has served as a missionary in Ethiopia; as campus pastor and religion professor at Dana College, Blair, Nebraska; and as professor of systematic theology at Wartburg Seminary, Dubuque, Iowa; and Luther Northwestern Seminary, St. Paul, Minnesota.

Contents

Preface   11

1   What Is God's Will for My Life?   13

2   How Can I Learn to Pray: Your Will Be Done?   21

3   How Can the Christian Community
    Help Me Make Decisions?   29

4   Why Me, Lord?   37

5   Why Is There Evil?   45

6   How Can I Be Released from Evil Powers?   53

7   Will God Be There for Me?   61

8   How Can I Cope?   69

9   Can God Heal Me?   77

10 How Shall We Live in a Nuclear World?   85

Preface

Some of life's questions continually haunt us. Research indicates that one of the questions which constantly surfaces among Christian people is the question of God's will for their lives. To the best of my knowledge, the question about God's will for our lives is the number one question that Christian people ask. Christians want to know how to live out their lives according to God's plans.

What Is God's Will for My Life? asks the title of this book. Three chapters are directed toward answering this question. I have used these as messages over my nationwide radio program. These were the most highly requested messages that I have ever given. I hope these chapters prove helpful for you as well.

There are other questions that haunt us. Can God heal me? How can I cope? How shall we live in a nuclear world? These and other vital questions will be addressed in following chapters with the help of biblical passages.

There are two temptations that arise in seeking to address the fundamental questions of human life. The first temptation is to resort to simple answers, quoting a Bible passage, for example, as if that would settle the matter once and for all. Very few of the critical questions that we ask can be answered that simply!

Simple answers that quote Scripture also run the risk of misusing Scripture. The fundamental purpose of Scripture is not to function as a kind of heavenly answer book for human questions. The fundamental purpose of Holy Scripture is to serve as *an instrument through which God comes to walk into our lives in Jesus Christ*. God's answer to our human dilemma is not so much *an idea that will instruct us* as it is God's offer in Jesus Christ to come as a *person and walk with us* through every night of darkness, until God brings us at last to eternal light and life.

A second temptation in dealing with these fundamental questions is to give no answers at all. One can assume that the questions we ask are so complex and so filled with ambiguity that no satisfactory answers can be given to them. When this approach is taken we are simply left to struggle with the questions as we live our lives of faith.

I have tried in these messages to avoid both of these temptations. I have tried to give some practical help in dealing with these crucial areas of life without being simplistic. My prayer is that the God who comes into our lives through the Scripture may come into your life through these chapters. My prayer is that you will experience the presence of God in Jesus Christ walking with you, and being personally present with you as you seek the guidance and help of God on your journey of faith.

1

What Is God's Will for My Life?

We know that in everything God works for good with those who love him, who are called according to his purpose. For those whom he foreknew he also predestined to be conformed to the image of his Son, in order that he might be the first-born among many brethren. And those whom he predestined he also called; and those whom he called he also justified; and those whom he justified he also glorified.

What then shall we say to this? If God is for us, who is against us? God did not spare God's own son but gave him up for us all; how shall God then give us all things, along with the Son? Who shall bring any charge against God's elect? It is God who justifies; who is to condemn? Is it Christ Jesus, who died, yes, who was raised from the dead, who is at the right hand of God, who indeed intercedes for us? Who shall separate us from the love of Christ? Shall tribulation, or distress, or persecution, or famine, or nakedness, or peril, or sword?

As it is written,
   "For your sake we are being killed
      all the day long;
   we are regarded as sheep to be
      slaughtered."
No, in all these things we are more than conquerors through
the one who loved us. For I am sure that neither death, nor
life, nor angels, nor principalities, nor things present, nor
things to come, nor powers, nor height, nor depth, nor
anything else in all creation, will be able to separate us from
the love of God in Christ Jesus our Lord.

Romans 8:28-39 (LCP)

"What should I do with my life?" Bob asked me in a pleading voice. I was a campus pastor at the time. He was a junior in college. "I've been taking mostly science courses," he told me. "I thought I wanted to be a biology teacher. But now I don't know. Maybe I should go to the seminary. Maybe I should be a pastor. I don't know what to think anymore. I've prayed about it, but it's just not clear to me. How can I know what is right? What is God's will for my life?" Bob's questions are very common questions raised by people of all ages: What is God's will for my life? How can I know what is right?

Mary Ann was in a dilemma. She was a widow. Her husband had died 10 years ago. Suddenly a couple of men came into her life. "What should I do?" she asked her closest friend, Beverly. "Am I supposed to get married again or not? What would be best for my children? What would be best for me? And toughest of all, which of these men is the right one for me? For goodness' sake, how are you supposed to decide these things? What is the right thing to do? What does God want me to do?"

George was in a dither. He and Ruth had been married

for five years. They were ready to start a family, and they thought they should move out of their apartment and buy a home of their own. "Buying a home sure is a big commitment," George said to his dad. "Do you think we can afford it? How much should we invest in a house? And which house is the best one? Ruth and I have looked at a lot of nice houses. I don't know how to decide. What is right for us, dad?"

These kinds of decisions face all of us at some point or another in our lives. Where shall we work? Whom shall we marry? Where shall we live? Besides these large questions about our lives, there are a multitude of smaller decisions that we face every day. How can we spend our time most wisely? How should we relate to those around us? How should we spend and invest our money? Is this action that I am contemplating right or wrong?

We make decisions about our lives all the time. Most of us are concerned that we make the right decisions. We want to know what is right for us. Christian people might say they want to live in God's will for their lives. How do we know God's will for our lives? What is God's will for my occupation and for my marriage and the many daily decisions that I face? Let us focus on what we know and what we do not know about living in God's will.

Let me take up the negative side first. What is it we do *not* know about God's will for our lives? The answer to that question is important. I maintain it is *very seldom we know God's plan for our lives in any detailed way.* I am not even sure God has such a plan for our lives. What we know of God is that which is revealed to us in Jesus Christ. *Jesus Christ is God's plan for our lives. God's will is that we experience God's love through Jesus Christ.* In and through the work of Jesus Christ we experience God's love for us; we experience a God who lives in us in spite of our sinfulness; we experience a God who embraces us in time and in eternity. God's love for sinful humanity is the heart of God's revelation for us in Jesus Christ. Our experience of that revelation, however, does not necessarily include a revelation of God's specific will for the living of our lives.

To be sure, there are examples, both in the Bible and in the life of the church, of people who have experienced the revelation of God's will for their lives. Abraham and Sarah had such an experience:

> The Lord had said to Abram, "Leave your country, your people and your father's household and go to the land I will show you. I will make you into a great nation and I will bless you; I will make your name great, and you will be a blessing. I will bless those who bless you, and whoever curses you I will curse; and all peoples on earth will be blessed through you.
>
> Genesis 12:1-3

God's call to Abraham and Sarah is clear and unmistakable.

Many of the prophets in the Old Testament had similar experiences of God's will being revealed for their lives. In the New Testament, the apostle Paul experienced the revealing of God's will as he traveled the road to Damascus. The Lord Jesus appeared to Paul on the road and called Paul into ministry to the Gentile world. God clearly revealed to the apostle Paul God's will for Paul's life.

Abraham. The prophets. The apostle Paul. God revealed in some detail to each of them God's will for their lives. We could give other examples as well. But these persons are really the *exceptions* to the rule. God simply does not reveal to most of us the divinely ordained plan for our lives, our marriages, our occupations, and so on. To ask about God's specific plan for our lives is to ask for something that will remain quite unknown and hidden from most of us. That means *there are many different directions we can go with our lives and still live within God's will for us!*

I have referred to the fact that we do not know God's specific plan and will for our lives. The fact that we do not know God's specific plan for us does not mean, however, that there is *nothing* we know about God's will for our lives. There are some important things we *do* know.

Firstly, *we know the framework of God's will for our lives in this world.* A lawyer of the Pharisees once asked Jesus a question to test him. His question was:

> "Teacher, which is the greatest commandment in the law?" Jesus replied: " 'Love the Lord your God with all your heart and with all your soul and with all your mind.' This is the first and greatest commandment. And the second is like it: 'Love your neighbor as yourself.' All the Law and the Prophets hang on these two commandments."
>
> Matthew 22:36-40

Love God and love your neighbor. Love God through the loving of your neighbor. That is how we read it in 1 John 4:20-21:

> If anyone says, "I love God," yet hates his brother, he is a liar. For anyone who does not love his brother, whom he has seen, cannot love God, whom he has not seen. And he has given us this command: Whoever loves God must also love his brother.

God reveals to us through Jesus Christ what our lives in this world are to be like. We know the general framework of God's will for our lives. That general framework is that we are called to love God and love our neighbor. All of the decisions that we make about our lives are framed within these two great commandments. Our lives are not our own to do with as we please. We are created and called to live outside of ourselves. We are called to love God by loving our neighbor. That is God's will for our lives. That is the framework in which our lives ought to be lived.

Secondly, *we know we live our lives under the canopy of God's forgiving love*. That is important. If we knew exactly God's plan for us each moment of our lives, the protection of God's forgiving love might not be necessary. We would know what to do and, hopefully, we would do it. But I have said that we do not always know God's will for us. As Paul puts it in his letter to the Corinthians, "We live by faith, not by sight" (2 Corinthians 5:7).

We live by faith, not by sight. What does it mean to live by faith? A story from the life of Martin Luther explains it. One of Luther's closest working associates was a man by the name of Philipp Melanchthon. One day Melanchthon came to Luther for his advice. Philipp did not know what to do in a given matter. He could not determine God's will for him. Consequently, he was not doing anything. Luther's advice to Melanchthon was simple: "Sin boldly," Luther told him, "and believe in Christ all the more boldly still."

Luther knew what it meant to live by faith. When you live by faith and not by sight, it means that you have to be bold in what you choose to do. In telling Melanchthon to "sin boldly," Luther was not counseling him to sin. He was counseling him to be bold to choose and to act even if he did not know which action was the so-called "right" action in the eyes of God. We must decide one way or the other, Luther was saying. We cannot be paralyzed in our decision making.

Thirdly, and finally, *we know that nothing can separate us from the love of God in Christ Jesus our Lord*. In Romans 8:28 we read: "We know that in everything God works for good with those who love him. . . . " God does not fix our paths in life. God does not have it all planned out for us. Under God's framework for life and under God's canopy of love, we seek to make the best kinds of decisions we can make in the living of our lives. God is present with us as we face these decisions. God is at work in the midst of our decisions. In a sense this passage tells us that *God is always working to make the best of our decisions.* That is really a marvelous comfort for us! God works to make the best of our choices in life. "We know that in everything God works for good with those who love him. . . ."

So it is that our weak attemps to know and to do God's will do not separate us from God. As people claimed by Jesus Christ and committed to Jesus Christ, we choose and we decide and we act. We act in the assurance that nothing can separate us from the love of Christ.

What is God's will for our lives? I have tried to point to things we do not know and to things we do know about doing God's will. Very few of us ever know in whole or in part God's precise will and plan for our lives. That is not part of what God reveals to us when God is made known to us in Jesus Christ.

Most important for each one of us, for each of us who really seek to do God's will, are the things we know. In seeking to do God's will for our lives, we know the framework in which our decisions ought to be made. We ought to choose those courses of action which best express our love of God and our love for our neighbor.

We know we live our lives under the canopy of God's forgiving love. We live by faith, not by sight. We boldly make choices in our lives, trusting in God's forgiveness in Jesus Christ all the more boldly still.

We know that nothing can separate us from the love of Christ. God is at work in our lives making the best of our decisions. We make our daily decisions trusting in God's presence in our lives. We make our daily decisions believing that neither height, nor depth, "nor anything else in all creation, will be able to separate us from the love of God in Christ Jesus our Lord."

2

How Can I Learn to Pray: Your Will Be Done?

They went to a place called Gethsemane, and Jesus said to his disciples, "Sit here while I pray." He took Peter, James and John along with him, and he began to be deeply distressed and troubled. "My soul is overwhelmed with sorrow to the point of death," he said to them. "Stay here and keep watch." Going a little farther, he fell to the ground and prayed that if possible the hour might pass from him. "Abba, Father," he said, "everything is possible for you. Take this cup from me. Yet not what I will, but what you will."

Then he returned to his disciples and found them sleeping. "Simon," he said to Peter, "are you asleep? Could you not keep watch for one hour? Watch and pray so that you will not fall into temptation. The spirit is willing, but the body is weak."

Once more he went away and prayed the same thing. When he came back, he found them sleeping, because their eyes were heavy. They did not know what to say to him.

Returning the third time, he said to them, "Are you still sleeping and resting? Enough! The hour has come. Look, the Son of Man is betrayed into the hands of sinners. Rise! Let us go! Here comes my betrayer!"

Mark 14:32-42

"Every day we prayed that God's will might be done," she said. Esther Svendson could hardly hold back the tears as she talked. She and her husband Albert and their son Ron had been through a kind of living hell. The Svendsons are Minnesota farmers. The land on which they live, the land from which they have wrested a living, has been in their family for three generations. The farm crisis in rural America, however, has brought an end to their family farm operation.

"Every day we prayed that God's will might be done," Esther said. They had faced a crisis about their future. She and her husband had farmed the land together for many years. In recent years their son Ron had been able to take over the operation of the farm. Albert and Esther were proud of their son. They were pleased to see the land stay in the family.

But Ron started farming the family land at the wrong time. Many rural Americans can tell you the same story. Interest rates were too high. The value of the land decreased. When that happened, there was less collateral for much needed loans. Prices for feed and fertilizer and seed and machinery went up and up and up while the prices they received for their products were going down. What were they to do?

Ron was an excellent manager of the family farm. The local banker said that he was one of the best managers he had ever met. When he came into the bank for a loan, he had computer print-outs of all the necessary information. "It was easy to do business with Ron," the banker said. Because Ron was such a good manager, he could see the crisis coming. As he plotted the next year at his computer, the figures that loomed before his eyes spoke a discouraging word. The projected profit could not meet the projected expenses. To continue the farm operation for another year would sink the family hopelessly in debt. Ron went over his figures with his parents. What were they going to do? "Every day we prayed that God's will might be done," Esther said.

Painfully, tearfully, they reached their decision. There would be a farm sale. But even that would not cover the debts. Half the land would have to be sold as well. And so it was done. On a cold winter's day, at a public auction, the Svendson family farm operation came to a close. "I really believe that we did God's will," Esther Svendson said.

We should not take Esther's words to mean that somehow from all eternity God had a plan that the Svendson family farm should be sold! By no means! It was not God's eternal will that a particular farm should be sold. We must be careful about how we assign the blame for things that happen in human life to the will of God. It is a rare occurrence for the God we meet in the Bible to *will* evil into human life. We need to remember that we live in a fallen world. Our world has fallen out of God's chosen course. Most evil that befalls us is a result of the sin-caused fall, not of God's will. I indicated in the first chapter that we *know* what the will of God is. God's will is that we might experience God's love through Jesus Christ. Esther Svend-son *believed* that the selling of the farm was an action consistent with God's overall care for her and her family.

What is God's will for my life? That is a question that many of us struggle with at many different periods of our lives. In the Lord's Prayer Jesus taught us to pray, "Your will be done." But how are we to know God's will? How do we do God's will? How do we know what is right for our lives? Part of the answer to these questions is prayer. We discern God's will for our lives through prayer.

Esther Svendson prayed throughout their ordeal with the farm. She *daily prayed* for God's will to be done. She believed what they chose to do was God's will. She believed it because the *events* surrounding her family *tended to confirm* that fact. The circumstances were that farm prices were going down and the cost of farming was going up. *Common sense* also led them in the direction of a farm sale. Ron Svendson's computer print-outs did not lie. They gave a clear indication of what the future would be. The doors seemed to be closed to a future in farming on this land at this time. And so they made a bold decision. They chose to have a sale. Esther saw it as God's will. "Your will be done." That was her constant prayer.

Esther Svendson is a helpful model for us as we seek out God's will for our lives. Prayer is probably the most important thing we can do in searching out God's will for our lives. God will lead us. That leading, however, will seldom come through a clear voice from heaven. Esther Svendson heard no such voice. But she could read the signs. She could see the circumstances. She could use her common sense. She could see the doors closing. She believed they had done God's will.

One other thing about the Svendsons. *They prayed.*

They sought to understand God's will and they believed they had done God's will. But that did not mean that it was easy. When Esther told me that she firmly believed they had done God's will, there were tears in her eyes and sorrow etched in her whole being.

Doing God's will for our lives can be painful. God does not always choose to lead us in pleasant paths. Sometimes God leads us through the valley of the shadows. God leads us at times through the darkness. But God's Son, Jesus Christ, won God's greatest victory in the darkness of Good Friday's crucifixion. We never, therefore, enter the darkness alone. Jesus Christ has entered the darkness ahead of us. Jesus Christ will be present with us in the darkness. Jesus Christ will shape us into his image in the darkness and walk with us into the eternal light of God.

The Lord Jesus taught us to pray. He taught us to pray that God's will be done in our lives. Jesus practiced what he preached. In the passage of Scripture from Mark's gospel that this chapter is based on, we read that Jesus was wrestling with God's will in prayer. Jesus walked with his disciples to Gethsemane. Jesus was greatly stressed and troubled. His soul was overwhelmed with sorrow to the point of death. He knew what lay ahead of him. The cup he was to drink was bitter. "*Abba*, Father," Jesus prayed, "everything is possible for you. Take this cup from me. Yet not what I will, but what you will." He prayed that prayer over and over again. Finally the matter was settled. His betrayer was near. Jesus went with the betrayer. He went to live out God's will for his life. He went to die.

"Take this cup from me," Jesus prayed. "Yet not what I will, but what you will. Your will be done." Prayer is our chief means of discovering God's will for our lives. We can take Jesus in Gethsemane's garden as our guide. Jesus' prayer instructs us that praying for God's will in our lives can be filled with distress. His prayer instructs us that praying for God's will in our lives is something we do over and over again. Jesus' prayer also instructs us that praying for God's will in our lives can be a mighty struggle between our will and God's will. And, finally, Jesus' prayer instructs us that praying for God's will in our lives may lead us to a time of suffering.

"Your will be done." That is how Jesus taught us to pray. It is in and through prayer more than any other activity that we come to understand God's will for our lives. There are many aspects of prayer, but perhaps the most fundamental purpose of prayer is to discern God's will for our lives. As people for whom Christ has died, we know that our lives no longer belong to us to do with as we please. Our lives belong to God. That is why we pray, "your will be done."

We close our prayers to God concerning God's will for us in Jesus' name. What we know of God, we know because God has been revealed to us in the person of Jesus of Nazareth. It is because we have been loved by God through Jesus that we want to offer our lives to God. We are also aware that Jesus is our great high priest who "always lives to intercede for [us]" (Hebrews 7:25b). We do not lift up our prayers in a vacuum. We are not alone in our praying. We pray in Jesus' name. We call upon God's Son to pray along with us, to pray for us. Such prayers shall surely be heard!

Prayer is not only our way of talking to God. *Prayer is also one of the ways that God talks to us.* Martin Luther once said that prayer is a conversation with God. In prayer we speak to God, and God speaks to us. As marvelous as it is that we have the opportunity to speak to God it is even more glorious that God speaks to us and that we may listen to

God. Luther felt that what God had to say to us is much more comforting than anything we have to say to God.

We pray, therefore, in order to hear God speak to us. We set aside time for listening. God may speak to us directly concerning God's will for our lives. It is important that we test such direct speaking of God with the Christian community. We should share God's directions to us with a Christian friend or with a pastor or with a prayer group or with our whole congregation. We do this to confirm God's direction for our lives. Checking our perception of God's will for our lives with others is of vital importance. We have our lives with God in community. We should treasure the guidance that the Christian community can give us.

There are other ways to confirm God's will for our lives. We need to be sensitive to the signs around us. What doors seem to be opening? What doors seem to be closing? What do our circumstances in life signal us? What does our common sense tell us? It is important to learn to read and heed these signs. Here, too, the help and guidance of Christian friends is crucial.

"Every day we prayed that God's will might be done," Esther Svendson said. The whole family prayed. Out of the covenant of their prayers, they made a bold decision. They chose to sell their machinery and half of their land. This was a difficult decision for them to make. But they had to choose.

That is true for all of us who seek to do God's will in our lives. We pray, "Your will be done." We pray in Jesus' name. We struggle in our prayers. We pray again and again. We listen to God for an answer. We consult other Christian people. We try to be sensitive to the signs, and, finally, we must make a bold decision of faith. In our decisions we are constantly aware that we walk by faith and not by sight. We trust that we have chosen God's will. It is not often, however, that we know for sure, that we know with absolute certainty that we have chosen rightly. Our comfort is that our lives are lived under God's mercy. We may not always make the wisest decision. *But God's love is greater than our decisions!* Good choices and bad, our lives are lived in safety under the canopy of God's forgiving love.

3

How Can the Christian Community Help Me Make Decisions?

"If your brother sins against you, go and show him his fault, just between the two of you. If he listens to you, you have won your brother over. But if he will not listen, take one or two others along, so that 'every matter may be established by the testimony of two or three witnesses.' If he refuses to listen to them, tell it to the church; and if he refuses to listen even to the church, treat him as you would a pagan or a tax collector.

"I tell you the truth, whatever you bind on earth will be bound in heaven, and whatever you loose on earth will be loosed in heaven.

"Again, I tell you that if two of you on earth agree about anything you ask for, it will be done for you by my Father in heaven. For where two or three come together in my name, there am I with them." Matthew 18:15-20

"Let's draw straws." Did you ever do that when you were young? I did. When we couldn't decide who should play what position in a baseball game, someone would usually say: "Let's draw straws." When we couldn't decide who should go first to ride the neighbor's horse, someone would usually say: "Let's draw straws." It was a way to help us kids make a difficult decision.

Not many of us would think that drawing straws is an acceptable method we could use to determine God's will for our lives. This method of making a decision, however, is not far from the way the eleven disciples of Jesus made a very important decision about God's will. We read in Acts 1:15-26 that the disciples felt led to replace the disciple who betrayed Jesus: Judas Iscariot. I cannot imagine a more important decision than that. Who would the new twelfth disciple be? Who would take the place of Judas?

The eleven determined that Judas's replacement should be a man who had accompanied them during Jesus' entire life and ministry. They selected the two best candidates. One was named Joseph Barsabbas, the other was named Matthias. Having put forward these two men, they prayed for God's guidance in their decision; they prayed to discern God's will in the matter.

> "Lord, you know everyone's heart. Show us which one of these two you have chosen to take over this apostolic ministry, which Judas left to go where he belongs."
>
> Acts 1:24-25

What happened next surprises me every time I read it. They cast lots. The disciples cast lots and the lot fell to Matthias. It is almost as if someone had said: "Let's draw straws." I always expect that the people in the Bible, and certainly Jesus' very own disciples, must have had a clear vision of God's will for their lives. I may not always be able to figure out God's will for my life, but surely the eleven disciples did not have that problem. But the fact of the matter is the disciples did have that problem! They struggled to know God's will for their lives just as we struggle to know and to do God's will.

The disciples prayed for God's will to be done. In the previous chapter I referred to the vital importance of prayer in determining God's will. The disciples prayed and then they cast lots. Casting lots was a fairly common custom in the Old Testament. We are not exactly sure how it was done, but God's people of old often cast lots as a way of discerning God's will. Casting lots and other similar practices were seen as God's way of speaking God's mind into the situation. Notice this passage from the Old Testament book of Proverbs:

"The lot is cast into the lap, but its every decision is from the Lord."

Proverbs 16:33

There is a passage in the gospel of Matthew that also applies to the situation of the disciples. In Matthew 18:15-20, the gospel writer tells us how the early Christian community was to resolve disputes between its members. The early Christian community clearly understood that Christ himself was present and acting with the church in the matter of resolving disputes. "For where two or three come together in my name," Jesus said, "there am I with them" (Matthew 18:20).

But the early church understood that Christ was with them in more ways than in resolving disputes. The eleven disciples who prayed that God would show them which one was to succeed Judas Iscariot believed that Jesus was present and acting with them in revealing God's will for their future. The eleven disciples faced a very crucial decision. They believed that when they gathered together in Jesus' name, when they gathered together in prayer, when they cast lots, Jesus was indeed with them.

We come, then, to a very important principle for determining God's will for our lives. That principle is: *Whenever possible, we ought to seek guidance from the Christian communty in determining God's will for our lives.* When faced with a decision in which we pray that God's will be done, we ought also to talk and pray with our Christian friends. We might consult with members of our own family, or with a counselor or a pastor. We might talk with someone whose wisdom we trust. In making important life decisions, in making decisions in which we pray that God's will might be done, we ought to openly seek the counsel of the Christian community. We know that Jesus is present and active in our lives when we gather together in his name with Christian friends to seek God's will for our lives.

It was the summer of my sixteenth year. I was not too pleased with my attitude toward God and the church. Therefore, when the pastor asked me to go to a leadership training event at a Bible camp, I jumped at the chance. *A week at Bible camp might just help turn me around*, I thought to myself. I went to camp with a good deal of anticipation.

It was a good week. Our teachers ware excellent. One young pastor was particularly forceful and impressive. The words of affirmation that he spoke to me were very important in my life's journey. One night at camp some of us read through a play for the other campers. I had a leading role. After the play, this young pastor publicly affirmed my dramatic skills. The other kids at camp were also affirming. I do not have to tell you how good that felt. We all like to be affirmed.

Privately, this young pastor was also affirming. He asked me if I had ever considered becoming a pastor. He told me that he thought the gifts I had could well be used in the ordained ministry. My conversation with this pastor played a very important role in my young life. If he had not talked with me, I don't know whether I would have chosen the ministry or not, but I do know that our conversation helped me as I sought to do God's will for my life. This pastor, and many other members of the Christian community, helped me discover what my gifts were and how those gifts might best be used. Other people, God's people, helped me discover God's will for my life.

I am not unique in this. I am sure that many of you have had similar experiences in sorting out God's will for your lives. You benefited from the advice of other people. You learned more about yourselves through the words of others. Various members of the Christian community helped you make an important decision about your lives. You have experienced that in your lives. I have experienced that in my life. Jesus Christ has helped us discern God's will through the counsel and advice and guidance of other people.

We continue to be confronted with difficult decisions in our lives. We continue to ponder what choices we can make that will best give expression to God's will for us. How are such decisions to be made? We need to be reminded that we should never try to determine in a vacuum God's will for our lives. We should not try to discern God's will when we are alone. After God had created Adam, God said, "It is not good for the man to be alone. I will make a helper suitable for him" (Genesis 2:18).

It is not good for us to be alone! Those words echo across the centuries. God's intention for our lives is that we live in community with other people. We begin our lives on earth in a family. We may later on choose to form our own family. We identify with the community of God's people called the church and with other forms of community as well. It is not good for us to be alone. We have been created *in* community. We have been created *for* community. We ought naturally look to our communities for help and guidance in the important decisions of our lives. Looking to the community of God's people is a fundamental way we have of determining God's will for our lives. In and through the Christian community, Jesus Christ himself is present for us. In and through the Christian community, Jesus Christ is active, helping to shape and form our decisions.

I want to conclude this chapter by posing a challenge to the question itself, "How can I know God's will for my life?" Christian people ask that question. We would like to know the answer to that question. But *are we asking the right question?* Can we really know—*know*, mind you!—God's will for each moment of our lives? Can we always or ever know God's precise will for our lives?

I do not think we can! That is not a problem with God. It's a problem with us. *Our sinfulness* has separated us from God. Paul the apostle says in 1 Corinthians 13:9 that our knowledge is imperfect. "Now we see but a poor reflection as in a mirror," he says. "Now I know in part" (verse 12). Or, as we have earlier quoted Paul, "We live by faith, not by sight" (2 Corinthians 5:7).

Luther gave some advice for Christians living by faith. "Sin boldly," Luther said. He meant that even though we cannot know in completeness what God's will for us might be, we must move forward in life, always imperfectly, making bold decisions about what we shall be and do. "Make bold decisions," Luther was saying, "and believe in Christ all the more boldly still."

Luther, in giving this advice, is simply agreeing with

the apostle Paul. We do only know in part. Our knowledge is imperfect. Therefore, we will almost always find ourselves choosing and acting out in uncertainty what we pray God's will for our lives to be. We do not know for sure. We are never absolutely certain. We will probably "sin boldly," making mistakes as we go. We choose anyway. We act anyway. We live in Christ's forgiveness.

We choose and we act in the absolute trust that God's canopy of love embraces our every step.

We choose and we act, believing in Christ more boldly than we believe in the rightness of our decisions.

We choose and we act, confident that Jesus Christ will walk with us every step of the way.

May Jesus Christ walk with you every step of your way as you earnestly seek to do God's will in your life.

4

Why Me, Lord?

Then the Lord answered Job out of the storm.
He said:

"Who is this that darkens my counsel
with words without knowledge?
Brace yourself like a man;
I will question you,
and you shall answer me.
"Where were you when I laid the
earth's foundation?
Tell me, if you understand.
Who marked off its dimensions? Surely
you know!
Who stretched a measuring line
across it?
On what were its footings set,
or who laid its cornerstone—
while the morning stars sang together
and all the angels shouted for joy?"

Job 38:1-7

Marilyn knelt at her husband's bedside. He was 42, he had cancer, and he was dying. She was afraid and full of questions. "What is happening to my husband?" she cried out in the darkness. "What is happening to me? How will we manage? Who will be father to my children?" She tried to collect her thoughts. She wanted to pray. But what could her prayer be? There was really only one thought that occupied her, that drove all other thoughts out of her mind. "Why me, Lord?" she pleaded over and over again. "Why is this happening to me?"

Life on the farm had been tough for Ed Russell. Land values had slipped. Interest rates were high. Costs for planting the fields continued to rise. But the prices that he got for his crops had stayed basically the same. It would take a good year just to break even. Ed Russell needed a good year, a very good year. Then it happened. There was a violent summer storm. When Ed checked his fields the next morning, he discovered that hail had seriously damaged half of his crops. And, what was worse, his was the only farm for miles around that suffered any hail damage from the storm. "Why?" Ed pleaded with no one in particular. "Why me, Lord? Why me?"

Peggy Flint hated her new school. She never wanted to leave her old school. It was nice there. She had friends; she was part of that school. But her dad got transferred and the whole family had to move. Peggy Flint did not like it. There were a lot of bad things about moving, but the worst was leaving her friends. That is what Peggy did not like about her new school. She had no friends there. She felt all alone. She was very lonely. "Why me, Lord?" Peggy's evening prayer began. "Why do I have to be so lonely?"

"Why me, Lord?" That is a common human prayer and cry. We have all said it many times. But we are not the first to raise this human cry. We are not the first to pray this simple prayer. Listen to this centuries-old prayer from the Psalms:

> Why, O Lord, do you stand far off?
> Why do you hide yourself in times of trouble?
>   Psalm 10:1

"Why me, Lord?" is an ancient and universal human prayer.

The most important biblical personality to challenge God with "Why?" questions was Job. In Job we really have a classic case of a righteous person who suffers much in life. That is what lies behind our "Why?" questions, isn't it? We ask "Why?" when we do not think we have deserved the suffering that we receive.

In the book of Job, Job's friends tried to answer his questions about his lot in life. What Job's friends told him is important for us to note. Job's friends tried to answer the "Why?" question for him. Their answers are as good as anyone can come up with to explain human suffering. I am sure that you have spoken and heard many of these answers yourself. Here are just a few of their answers to Job's question "Why?"

"Consider now," said Eliphaz, "Who, being innocent, has ever perished? Where were the upright ever destroyed?" (Job 4:7).

Eliphaz continued, "Blessed is the man whom God corrects; so do not despise the discipline of the Almighty" (Job 5:17).

Bildad, another friend, added his answer: "Does God pervert justice? Does the Almighty pervert what is right?" (Job 8:3).

The answers of Job's friends continued. And they are pretty good answers. Most of them make some sense; we have used them ourselves. But Job would hear nothing of them. He rejected every answer. He grew angry with his friends. He cursed the day of his birth. He demanded an audience with God. Surely God knew that he, Job, had not deserved his suffering!

Let us look again at a couple of lines from God's answer to Job. Job asked "Why? Why me, Lord?" and God says, "Where were you when I laid the earth's foundation? Tell me, if you understand. Who marked off its dimensions? Surely you know!" (Job 38:4-5).

God's speech to Job continued. God told Job of the many mysteries of the created order that are in God's hand alone. Job knew very little of God's way in the world. The summary of God's speech to Job could well be those words of God that we read in Isaiah 55:8-9:

> "For my thoughts are not your thoughts, neither are your ways my ways," declares the Lord. "As the heavens are higher than the earth, so are my ways higher than your ways and my thoughts than your thoughts."

"My thoughts are not your thoughts. My ways are not your ways." That is God's basic answer to Job. And Job repented. He did not get a clear answer to his "Why?" questions. But Job had met God. God had come to meet Job right in the middle of Job's human dilemma.

So it must be with us. We ask our questions. "Why me, Lord?" We cry out to God. But God has no simple answers for our questions. God's thoughts are not our thoughts. God's ways with this created order are far too complex for us to understand. According to the story of Job, God does not engage in answering our "Why?" questions.

I talked with a couple a few years ago whose child was

born with Down's syndrome. They had no idea that such a thing would happen to them. They had no warning. The delivery room was supposed to be a joyful place—it quickly became a place of dread. The parents were in shock. And you know what they said, "Why me, Lord?"

Like Job, they had lots of friends with lots of answers to their "Why?" questions. They were answers they themselves had offered to others in the past. But suddenly those answers all sounded hollow. None of the answers they heard were helpful. They lived in a state of turmoil until one of them finally asked a new question. "Why not? We live in a world of pain," the wife said to me. "God has not made us exempt from pain."

From that moment on this couple began to deal realistically with the opportunity that lay before them. "Why not?" That is a good question, a revolutionary question. It is a question that acknowledges that, indeed, God's thoughts and God's ways are not our ways. There are ways, I think, that this prayer, this "Why not?" prayer, is the prayer we learn from the experience of Job.

God did not answer Job's question. But God met Job in the midst of his circumstances. God met Job; God accepted Job's repentance; and God restored Job's fortunes. God met Job in the midst of Job's suffering. But that was not the last time, that was not the only time, that God has come to meet us in the midst of human suffering. God became flesh and dwelt among us. God came to live in the midst of our circumstances. God came to dwell with us in Jesus Christ. In and through the life of Jesus Christ, God has lived the "Why?" question.

Jesus was rejected by the religious leaders of his day. They rejected him with the intent of killing him. Their killing plans came true. Jesus of Nazareth was nailed to a criminal's cross and hung to die. Jesus protested his dying.

He protested directly to God. "My God, my God, why have you forsaken me?" Jesus cried out from his cross of death. "Why me, Lord?" Jesus prayed on the cross. Jesus prayed our prayer! Jesus knows what it means to ask, "Why?" Jesus understands our prayers. We could almost say that Jesus is the one who has taught us the "Why me?" prayer!

There is an answer to our "Why me, Lord?" prayer. God's answer to our prayer is a person. Our answer from God is Jesus Christ. Jesus Christ has prayed that prayer with us. Jesus Christ is one with us as we hurl out our questions to God. Jesus Christ participates with us in our desperate cry. *Our prayers are made legitimate by the cross of Christ.* God understands human suffering. God understands our pain. God understands our questioning prayer. The God of the cross lives on intimate terms with our human bewilderment.

If Jesus Christ, the Son of God, could cry out his "Why?" to God, we can cry out with him. Was his prayer answered by God? Yes and no. First the "no." There is no place in the Bible where God specifically answers this question. But, yes, God does answer Jesus' prayer. God answers Jesus' prayer by lifting him from the cross, raising him from the grave, and granting him eternal life.

It is this Jesus Christ, this risen-from-the-cross-and-grave Jesus Christ, who is the answer to our prayers. "Why me, Lord?" we cry. Does God answer our prayer? Yes and no. First the "no." As with Job and Jesus, so with us, God does not always specifically answer our questioning prayers. God's thoughts are not our thoughts. But, yes, God does answer our prayers. God answers our prayers through a person. God answers our prayers through our crucified and risen Lord Jesus Christ.

Jesus Christ, crucified and risen, says to us this day: "I have participated in your prayers of bewilderment. I know your human yearnings. I know the taste of your suffering. I also know the taste of suffering transformed into joy.

"I was lifted from my cross. I was raised from my grave. I offer this day to walk with you.

"I will walk with you in your anguish. You will walk with me in my joy. We will walk together, you and I.

"I will walk with you through suffering and death. I will also walk with you in resurrection and life. I will walk with you for eternity.

"Take my hand. Let us walk an eternal walk together."

5

Why Is There Evil?

A few days later, when Jesus again entered Capernaum, the people heard that he had come home. So many gathered that there was no room left, not even outside the door, and he preached the word to them. Some men came, bringing to him a paralytic, carried by four of them. Since they could not get to Jesus because of the crowd, they made an opening in the roof above Jesus and, after digging through it, lowered the mat the paralyzed man was lying on. When Jesus saw their faith, he said to the paralytic, "Son, your sins are forgiven."

Now some of the teachers of the law were sitting there, thinking to themselves, "Why does this fellow talk like that? He's blaspheming! Who can forgive sins but God alone?"

Immediately Jesus knew in his spirit that this was what they were thinking in their hearts, and he said to them, "Why are you thinking these things? Which is easier: to say to the paralytic, 'Your sins are forgiven,' or to say, 'Get up, take your mat and walk'? But that you may know that the Son of Man has authority on earth to forgive sins. . . ." He said to the paralytic, "I tell you, get up, take your mat and go home." He got up, took his mat and walked out in full view

of them all. This amazed everyone and they praised God,
saying, "We have never seen anything like this!"
Mark 2:1-12

Fires burned out of control all over the western United
States one summer. The roar of flames consumed human
life, valuable property, and countless acres of vegetation.
News reports said there was suspicion of arson in some of
the fires. Perhaps someone had set these fires. We wondered
at the very thought. Why would anyone do such a thing?
Why is there such evil in the world?

The storm came up almost without warning. The sky
turned dark and foreboding. Funnels of clouds formed in
the atmosphere. Tornadoes unleashed their fury. Several
cities stood in their path. The extent of the destruction was
almost unbelievable. Has nature itself gone berserk? We
hear such reports with annual predictability. We wonder at
the mystery of it all.

Stories of political repression appear with regularity on
the evening news. There are governments in our world that
systematically and ruthlessly suppress their people. The stories of torture bewilder us. How can human beings treat
other human beings in such inhuman ways? Why is there
evil in the world?

The first biblical passage that takes up the question of
evil in the world is in the book of Genesis, the first book
in the Bible, Chapter 3. Adam and Eve were alive in God's
good world. Then the serpent entered. Who the serpent was
we do not know; we are not told. We do know the serpent's
mission. The serpent's mission was to tempt Eve and Adam
to put their own lives ahead of God's will for them. The
serpent said to Eve, "Did God really say, 'You must not
eat from any tree in the garden'?" (Genesis 3:1b).

Eve replied that God had not said that. "We may eat

fruit from the trees in the garden, but God did say, 'You must not eat fruit from the tree that is in the middle of the garden, and you must not touch it, or you will die' " (Genesis 3:2-3).

"You will not surely die," the serpent said to the woman. "For God knows that when you eat of it your eyes will be opened, and you will be like God, knowing good and evil" (Genesis 3:4-5).

The serpent's words lay before us what is perhaps the most fundamental of all human temptations. This is a temptation that seduces our pride, seduces our ego, seduces our sense of independence. We can be like God! We can be the center of our own world—the god of our own lives. We can be the master of our own destiny. Eve and Adam fell for that temptation. They reached for the tree to be like God. The God who created heaven and earth was no longer their God, was no longer the center of their world. Eve became the center of her world. Adam became the center of his world. That was their sin. That is the sin of the entire human race that follows in this rebellious path of our first parents.

The story of Adam and Eve is not just a once-upon-a-time story. It is *a story of what life in time is like.* The story of Eve and Adam is not just the story of how sin was original in the first humans. It is the story of how sin is original in every human being. This story is our story. *We have rebelled against God.* You and I have rebelled against God. We have chosen to be like God in our own lives. We have chosen to be the masters of our own destiny; to be the center of our own worlds. We have made our declaration of independence from God. "There is no one righteous, not even one," the apostle Paul wrote in Romans 3:10.

That is *part of the reason* why there is evil in the world. *There is evil in the world because the world is populated with sinful people.* Human beings put their own desires ahead of

God's desire for them. You and I are sinful people; we are sinful people who bring evil to God's world.

And God punishes sinful people. We read that in the last half of Genesis 3. God cursed the serpent. God cursed the woman:

> I will greatly increase your pains in childbearing; with pain you will give birth to children. Your desire will be for your husband, and he will rule over you.
>
> Genesis 3:16

God cursed the man:

> Because you have listened to your wife, and ate from the tree about which I commanded you, 'You must not eat of it,' cursed is the ground because of you; through painful toil you will eat of it all the days of your life; it will produce thorns and thistles for you; and you will eat the plants of the field. By the sweat of your brow you will eat your food until you return to the ground, since from it you were taken; for dust you are and to dust you will return.
>
> Genesis 3:17-19

God's curse hangs heavy over a world where human beings have rebelled against their Creator. That is one way the Bible has of telling us how we, how Eve and Adam and you and I, have brought a curse, have brought evil into our world through our rebellious pride. The prophet Hosea had another way of telling us how evil spreads in the world. God spoke through the prophet. God spoke of the evil works of the people of Israel. God said: Their sins engulf them; they are always before me" (Hosea 7:2b).

It is as if our sinful deeds send out a net of evil that traps people in its web. We are engulfed by our deeds! That is also what is meant by the repeated Old Testament admonition of God that God is a jealous God, ". . . punishing the children for the sin of the fathers to the third and fourth generation . . ." (Exodus 20:5).

That statement has sometimes troubled me. It doesn't seem quite fair of God to punish children and grandchildren for their parent's sin. We can look at this statement another way, however. We can hear it as a simple statement of the way things actually work in our world. All the data we can gather, for example, tells us that children abused by their parents will most probably abuse their children. Children of an alcoholic parent have a high percentage chance of themselves becoming alcoholics. Children born to mothers who abuse their own bodies during pregnancy with drugs or alcohol or tobacco are increasingly likely to be born with certain defects. I could give many other examples. That is just the way life is. Our deeds do engulf us. The sins of parents often do have consequences for their children.

When we turn to the New Testament, we hear the realities we have been discussing stated in another way. We have become slaves of sin, Paul the apostle tells us in Romans 6. Paul describes the nature of sin as a power at work in our lives. Sin is a power that can enslave us. Sin is a power that can reign in our bodies. Sin is a power that can bring death to human life: "the wages of sin is death" (Romans 6:23). Paul clearly understands that sin reigns in your life and in my life. When sin reigns in our lives, we are driven to actions that further unleash evil into our world.

These are some of the ways that the Bible has of coming to terms with the question of evil. Based on this brief look at some passages of Scripture, we can say the following:

First of all, there is evil in the world because Eve and Adam and you and I want to be like God. We are sinful human beings that put our will for our lives ahead of God's will for our lives. In other words, there is evil in the world because we are sinful people.

Secondly, there is evil in the world because God has punished our sinfulness with a curse on human life and on the world of nature. There is evil in the world because our sins form a net that traps us in a web. Our deeds engulf us. The sins of the parents ensnare their children.

Thirdly, there is evil in the world because sin has become a power that reigns over us, producing a world that is bound to death.

I have painted a rather bleak picture of a world ruled by the evil that comes into being through our human sinfulness. It is time to bring a word of hope into this picture. Enter Jesus of Nazareth! In Mark's gospel, this Jesus entered the world of a paralytic man. Friends of the paralytic carried him to Jesus, opened a hole in the roof of the house where Jesus was teaching, and lowered him at Jesus' feet. Friends of this man hoped for a miracle of healing. Jesus saw the man. Jesus saw the faith of the man's friends. Jesus spoke to the paralytic: "Son, your sins are forgiven."

Everyone was stunned by Jesus' words. The friends of the paralytic had not come for this! They came for a word of healing. The scribes, on the other hand, thought that Jesus had committed blasphemy. "Who can forgive sins but God alone?" they asked. Jesus replied to the scribes:

"Which is easier to say, 'Your sins are forgiven,' or to say, 'Get up and walk'? But so that you may know that the Son of Man has authority on earth to forgive sins. . . . Then he said to the paralytic, "Get up, take your mat and go home."
Matthew 9:5-6

Jesus had the authority on earth to forgive sins. Jesus came to this world with a mission from God. Part of that mission was the authority to forgive sinners. Jesus' mission of forgiveness was a mission that struck at the *root* of the human dilemma. Jesus saw the physical need of the paralytic. His first word to the paralytic, however, was not a word to this man's diseased body. Jesus saw that this diseased body was a symptom of a deeper human problem. As we have seen in our brief biblical overview, it is our human sinfulness that is at the root of the evil that pervades our world. A word of healing spoken to the paralytic would be a word spoken only to a symptom. Jesus knew that. So he addressed the *root cause* of human disease. "Son," Jesus said, "your sins are forgiven."

The Bible helps to give us an answer to the question of why there is evil in the world. But the God of the Bible is interested in something far more important than simply providing us with an abstract answer to the question of evil. God wills to give us a *personal response* to the evil that has come to rule our lives. God wills to give us God's Son to bring us a word that can drive evil out of human life.

There is evil in the world because you and I want to be like God. There is evil in the world because Eve and Adam and you and I are sinful human beings.

Evil is in the world because God has punished us with a curse. But Jesus Christ has taken our punishment upon himself. Jesus Christ has been cursed in our place.

There is evil in the world because our sins create a web that ensnares us. But Jesus of Nazareth frees us from sin's web.

Evil is in the world because sin has become a power that reigns over us. But sin has no power over Jesus Christ; he broke sin's stranglehold on human life.

In each of these, Jesus of Nazareth, the one person who has triumphed over sin, death, and evil, says to us: "My child, your sins are forgiven."

We understand, Lord, that a fundamental cause of evil in the world is a result of our sinful rebellion. We are sinful people, Lord. Our lives produce much that is evil. We are thankful that you came into our world and brought God's word of forgiveness into our lives. We pray that your word of forgiveness will penetrate deep into our lives and make new persons out of us, driving evil out of our lives. In your name we pray, Amen.

6

How Can I Be Released from Evil Powers?

Then Jesus was led by the Spirit into the desert to be tempted by the devil. After fasting forty days and forty nights, he was hungry. The tempter came to him and said, "If you are the Son of God, tell these stones to become bread."

Jesus answered, "It is written: 'Man does not live on bread alone, but on every word that comes from the mouth of God.'"

Then the devil took him to the holy city and had him stand on the highest point of the temple. "If you are the Son of God," he said, "throw yourself down. For it is written: 'He will command his angels concerning you, and they will lift you up in their hands, so that you will not strike your foot against a stone.'"

Jesus answered him, "It is also written: 'Do not put the Lord your God to the test.'"

Again, the devil took him to a very high mountain and showed him all the kingdoms of the world and their splendor.

*"All this I will give you," he said, "if you will bow down
and worship me."*

*Jesus said to him, "Away from me, Satan! For it is
written: 'Worship the Lord your God, and serve him only.' "
Then the devil left him, and angels came and attended him.*
Matthew 4:1-11

"The devil made me do it!" Have you ever heard that
or said it? Some years ago, that line was popularized on Flip
Wilson's comedy television show. It became a standard line
that would pop up anytime one of Mr. Wilson's characters
made a wrong turn. "Why am I doing what I'm doing?"
the character would ask. "The devil made me do it."

In the previous chapter, I traced the origin of evil to
the root of our human sinfulness. There is evil in this world
because we are sinful and rebellious people. That is part of
the answer to the question of the origin of evil. It is not the
whole answer, however. When we talk of evil in the world,
we must also recognize that the Bible tells us that human
beings are contending "against the rulers, against the authorities, against the powers of this dark world and against
the spiritual forces of evil in the heavenly realms" (Ephesians 6:12b). The one-word name that the Bible often gives
us for these powers of darkness is the same name that Flip
Wilson used, that is, the devil.

The scripture reading from Matthew 4 is about a con-
flict between the devil and Jesus. *The Spirit led Jesus* into
the desert to be tempted by the devil. There is something
very important to notice here. The devil is not treated as a
power equal to God. The Spirit turned Jesus over to the
devil for a time of tempting and testing. The devil's power
is clearly kept within boundaries. *The devil is not one of two
equal powers* in the universe battling it out with God for

supremacy over people's lives. In the Bible it is almost always the case that the power of evil, the power of the devil, is a power that is limited by God. The power of evil certainly exists and cannot be taken lightly. The devil's power, however, is never equal to God's power.

The devil is described for us in many different ways in Scripture. In 1 Peter 5:8, for example, we read: "Be self-controlled and alert. Your enemy the devil prowls around like a roaring lion looking for someone to devour." In John 8:44 we read that the devil is the father of lies. There is no truth in the devil. Those persons under the devil's influence are, as Dr. Scott Peck puts it in his book of that title, *People of the Lie.*

We have some insight, therefore, into how the devil works in the world. But who is the devil anyway? Where has the devil come from? *It would be satisfying* to know the answer to that question, *but it is not possible.* The Bible simply does not answer that question. There has been a saying in the Christian church, for example, that the devil is a fallen angel. Two Old Testament passages used to support this idea are Isaiah 14:12-21 and Ezekiel 28:1-19.

In the Isaiah passage the *king of Babylon* is described as one fallen from heaven. In the Ezekiel passage the *king of Tyre* is described as having been in Eden, the garden of God. But God cast this king off God's mountain, "and I expelled you, O guardian cherub, from among the fiery stones" (Ezekiel 28:16b). To make these passages refer to the devil, we would have to ignore the fact that the passages themselves say they are talking about earthly kings and princes.

The fact remains that *we do not know* who the devil is or where the devil has come from. What we know *from our experience* in life is that evil is a mighty power in our lives and in the lives of others. We know the reality of evil even though we may not know the origin of evil.

Though we may not be able to name the origin of evil in our world, we are certainly aware of the many-sided face of evil. There is one face of evil in the world that becomes clearer to me each year. It is the evil that is enmeshed in some of the structures of human society. One can look at a country like South Africa and see the evil structure of that nation. What is called *apartheid* is part of that structure. The system of *apartheid* is a system that keeps the black citizens of that nation *apart*. It keeps them apart from the world of the ruling white society and condemns them to an oppressed existence. When people are oppressed in a society solely because of the color of their skin, we are confronted with a political structure that does evil to people. The black people of South Africa are "sinned against" by the South African political system.

It is easy for me to see evil in the structure of a nation so far away. It is harder for me to see the presence of evil in my own land. We have taken some major steps to assure justice for all, but the sin of racism has not disappeared. Many black people, many native American people, and many newly arrived immigrant people are trying to tell us yet today that being a nonwhite person in our society can be an oppressive reality. People are still "sinned against" in America because of the color of their skin. Are there structures of our society that unleash evil on people who do not fit the dominant category of our common life?

Other groups in our society also claim to be oppressed by our structures. Listen to the cry of the poor among us. By our government's own calculations, we know that the number of people living below the poverty line in our country has increased markedly over the last several years. What is most shocking about these figures is that the number of children living in poverty in our land has grown alarmingly. At the very same time, however, our nation has dramatically increased its spending on military hardware. Former President Dwight D. Eisenhower once said:

> Every gun that is made, every warship launched, every rocket fired, signifies in the final sense a theft from those who hunger and are not fed, those who are cold and are not clothed.

President Eisenhower's words seem to be coming true before our eyes. The increasingly military nature of our society has led to structures that oppress poor people.

Similar circumstances can be found throughout our world today. The nations of the world spend $800 billion a year for military purposes. At the same time, 43,000 children in the world die each day from lack of food and proper health care. There is something wrong with those priorities. The very structures of our societies become for us a sign of the presence of evil in our world. Our structures "sin against" powerless people.

It is my firm belief that structures of human society that bring evil results to people's lives are part of the rulers and authorities, the powers of this dark world, that Paul speaks of in Ephesians 6. The devil prowls around seeking to gain control of the very structures of human life. The power of evil in the world, the power of the devil, is a mighty power, a power that seems to render us helpless.

We need help, lots of help, to be able to withstand the assault of evil on our lives. The good news is we have such a helper—Jesus Christ. Jesus was led into the wilderness by God's Spirit in order to be tempted by the devil. The devil tempted a hungry Jesus by coaxing him to turn stones into bread. "Man does not live on bread alone . . . ," Jesus replied. The devil tempted Jesus by telling him to cast himself down from the highest point of the Temple. "God's angels will surely protect you," the devil said. But Jesus replied, "Do not put the Lord your God to the test." Finally, the devil invited Jesus to fall down and worship. "I'll give you all the kingdoms of the world and their splendor," the devil promised. Jesus replied: "Away from me, Satan! For it is written: 'Worship the Lord your God, and serve him only.' "

"Away from me, Satan!" That is Jesus' final word to the devil. *And the devil left Jesus.* The devil had no power over him! All the beguiling charms of the evil one could not seduce the Lord Jesus. But the devil does not give up easily. This Jesus had to be stopped; he had to be destroyed. So the rulers and powers of this dark world lined up against Jesus. The spiritual forces of evil conspired together to do him in. Evil powers sought to destroy Jesus and they succeeded—at least they thought they had succeeded. Jesus was nailed on a cross and left to die. How the devil and the devil's cohorts must have cheered at the sight!

Their evil cheers, however, were short-lived. The cross was not the end of this Jesus of Nazareth. Death itself, the last great power of the devil, could not contain him. Jesus rose from death and the grave. In so doing, Paul writes to the Colossians, Jesus "disarmed the powers and authorities, and made a public spectacle of them, triumphing over them by the cross" (Colossians 2:15).

Jesus faced the devil in the wilderness and Jesus sent him away empty-handed. "Away from me, Satan!" Jesus said. Jesus faced the rulers and authorities of this dark world on the cross and triumphed over them. *Jesus is God's revelation to all of us of God's answer to the problem of evil in the world. God in Jesus Christ has destroyed the devil's power.* God in Jesus Christ has triumphed over the rulers and authorities, has triumphed over the powers of this dark world, has triumphed over the spiritual forces of evil in the heavenly realms.

We need help to withstand the assault of evil upon our lives, to survive against the rulers and authorities at work in this world. We need help in order to withstand the evil that rules in the world through the very structures of human life. We need Jesus Christ who is our helper. Jesus Christ has come to set us free from the devil and all the devil's power.

The rulers and authorities of this world seek to enslave you. Jesus Christ has triumphed over these powers by the cross. Jesus Christ sets you free to live a fully human life.

The devil prowls around seeking to devour you. "Away, Satan!" Jesus says. Jesus Christ will protect you from the prowling of the enemy.

The father of lies wills to make liars out of us. The devil does not want us to be able to tell the truth that we need a Savior. The devil wants us to be "people of the lie." Jesus Christ has come that we can be people of the truth, people who need a Savior and praise God for sending one.

Evil powers infect the structures of human life which oppress the lives of people throughout the world. Jesus Christ has made a public example of such powers. Jesus Christ invites us to work for structures of human life that bring dignity to every human life and give us the courage to do so.

"Away, Satan!" That is the liberating word of Jesus Christ for you this day.

We hear your word of liberation, Lord Jesus. We hear and we believe. Let your liberating word so live within us that we are set free from the fear of evil's power. As persons liberated from the devil, make us people of the truth and give us the courage to fight to root out evil in the structures of human life and wherever else evil may be found. We pray in the reality of your liberating power. Amen.

7

Will God Be There for Me?

Give thanks to the Lord, for he is good.
His love endures forever.
Give thanks to the God of gods.
His love endures forever.
Give thanks to the Lord of lords:
His love endures forever.
to him who alone does great wonders,
His love endures forever.
who by his understanding made the heavens,
His love endures forever.
who spread out the earth upon the waters,
His love endures forever.
who made the great lights—
His love endures forever.
the sun to govern the day,
His love endures forever.
the moon and stars to govern the night,
His love endures forever.

to him who struck down the firstborn of Egypt
    His love endures forever.
and brought Israel out from among them
    His love endures forever.
with a mighty hand and outstretched arm;
    His love endures forever.
to him who divided the Red Sea asunder,
    His love endures forever.
and brought Israel through the midst of it,
    His love endures forever.
but swept Pharaoh and his army into the Red Sea;
    His love endures forever.
to him who led his people through the desert,
    His love endures forever.
who struck down great kings,
    His love endures forever.
and killed mighty kings—
    His love endures forever.
Sihon king of the Amorites
    His love endures forever.
and Og king of Bashan—
    His love endures forever.
and gave their land as an inheritance,
    His love endures forever.
an inheritance to his servant Israel;
    His love endures forever.
to the One who remembered us in our low estate,
    His love endures forever.
and freed us from our enemies,
    His love endures forever.
and who gives food to every creature,
    His love endures forever.
Give thanks to the God of heaven,
    His love endures forever.

                                  Psalm 136

The doors slammed shut behind Chaplain Gray. Chaplain Gray was a prison chaplain. He had grown accustomed to the feeling of being locked inside his prison-ministry home. It was a scary feeling for him, and the fear never quite left him.

One of his visits this day would be to Chuck Knowlton. Chuck had done it all; robbery, extortion, murder. Chuck had been in prison for a long time. He had a lot of time to think over the misdeeds of his youth. He appeared to be genuinely sorry for his life of crime. Chaplain Gray visited Chuck Knowlton regularly. Just about every time that he visited with him, Chuck would ask the same question, "Chaplain Gray," he would say with a look of deep sorrow, "have I committed the unforgivable sin?"

Chaplain Gray sought to assure him of God's grace and mercy. His words did not seem to have much effect on Chuck. The next time he would visit with him Chuck would ask the same question, "Have I committed the unforgivable sin? Can God, will God, really be there for me?" The question came out of Chuck Knowlton's deep sense of anxiety about himself. We know, you and I, the sense of anxiety that accompanies that question. "Will God be there for me?"

Shawn Kerry and Michelle O'Roarke were very close friends. They were the best of friends. Michelle was stunned, therefore, to hear that Shawn had walked out on her husband. She had just called on the telephone to say she was on her way over. Michelle paced the floor as she awaited Shawn's arrival.

Finally, there was a knock on the door. Shawn came in and sat down. She had been crying and looked exhausted. "I just couldn't take it anymore," Shawn began. "I've had it with that man. Now that the kids are grown, I'd like to go back to school and start a career, start a life of my own. He won't even discuss the possibility. When I bring it up, he just screams at me that I'm supposed to stay home where I belong. He beats me, too. It's getting worse, especially when he's been drinking. I can't take that abuse anymore. I'm going to file for divorce."

Michelle had listened quietly. There was a pause in the conversation. She did not know what to say. Shawn broke the silence. "I never thought I would even consider divorce. It certainly goes against all of my religious beliefs. What am I supposed to do? Let the man beat me to death? I won't let that happen. It makes me feel guilty, but I just don't know what else to do. What do you think, Michelle? Will God forgive me? Will God be there for me?" We know, you and I, the sense of guilt that accompanies questions like this.

Thad Blocker was late. He tried to get to the hospital every afternoon by three o'clock, but this day he was running behind schedule. Anita Blocker, Thad's mother, noted his delay. She had been in the hospital for two weeks now. The doctor said she had cancer—inoperable cancer. He said she only had a few weeks to live. What shock waves the doctor's words sent through Anita Blocker and her family! Who could have dreamed that such a thing could happen—and so suddenly!

Thad finally arrived at his mother's bedside. "You're late," she scolded in the way only a parent can do.

"How are you feeling today?" Thad said, hoping to divert attention from his tardiness.

"Not very well," his mother responded more weakly. "I don't feel well at all. Come here, son. Let me hold your hand. Can you feel my hands? Can you tell how weak I am? I don't have long, not long at all. I'm afraid. I'm afraid of dying. I don't want to die. What does it mean, anyway? Will God be there for me when I die, Thad?" There was fear in Anita Blocker's eyes as she spoke to her son. We know that fear, don't we. We know the fear that asks: Will God be there for me? Will God be there for me even in the hour of my dying?

We have heard a similar question on the lips of three people. We can identify with these people. We resonate to their questions. Out of our anxiety, out of our sense of guilt, out of our fear, we have asked and continue to ask similar questions. Will God be there for me? is a very common question, but it is a question which is out of focus because it is a self-centered question. It worries too much about *me*. The question presupposes that my relation to God is founded upon certain *conditions*. The question tends to presuppose that I am always vulnerable, always insecure, before God. If I do not do my part in life, if I do not live up to God's expectations for me, if I do not meet life's conditions, surely God will not be there for me.

That is how we think. Such thinking comes naturally to us, but often fails to hear the Bible's testimony to God's *unconditional* love. We think *conditionally*. Surely God's relationship to me is conditioned by the way I have related to God. When I fail to meet those conditions, I can only wonder. Out of my anxiety, out of my guilt, out of my fear, I wonder if God will really be there for me.

The biblical passage on which this chapter is based bears powerful witness to the unconditional and everlasting love of God for us:

> Give thanks to the Lord, for God is good,
>   God's love endures forever.
> Give thanks to the God of gods.
>   God's love endures forever.
> Give thanks to the Lord of lords,
>   God's love endures forever.
>   Psalm 136:1-3 (paraphrased)

These are just the first three verses of the psalm. It

goes on like that for 26 verses! Every verse ends with the same refrain: "God's love endures forever." Imagine yourself reciting this psalm with a congregation of God's people. Over and over the refrain resounds in your ears. Again and again the words are spoken or sung: "God's love endures forever." After 26 verses of that, you ought to experience the power of that word deep within your being.

The psalm shifts our attention away from ourselves and onto God. The psalm proclaims the nature of God for all to hear and know. "Will God be there for me?" we ask out of our self-centered insecurity. The psalmist seeks to drive our focus away from the nature of our fear-filled question and onto the nature of God. "Will God be there for me?" The answer is clearly a resounding YES! "God's love endures forever." God's steadfast love encompasses our lives.

It was the eternal and steadfast love of God hymned by the psalmist that became incarnate among us, that became flesh and dwelt among us, in Jesus Christ. Jesus Christ is God's love embodied in a person. For God so loved the world that God gave the Son, that whoever believes in him should not perish but have eternal life.

In Jesus Christ God's steadfast love could act and speak. One day Jesus spoke a parable, a parable of a prodigal son. This son took his inheritance from his father and went to live in a far country. He squandered his inheritance through foolish living. He wound up feeding pigs in order to stay alive. And while he slaved away among the pigs, he thought about his father's house. His father's hired servants were better off than he! So he decided to return to his home. He wondered about such a return. Would his father welcome him or throw him out? He figured his father's love was *conditional* love. If the son met the proper conditions, surely his father would welcome him.

The prodigal son set out for home prepared to meet

his father's conditions. He would repent before his father. He would say he was no longer worthy to be called his father's son. He would ask to be treated as a hired servant. "Surely if I meet these conditions," the prodigal son thought, "my father will be there for me." But the prodigal son was wrong, terribly wrong. His father's love for him was not conditional at all. *His father loved him without conditions.* "Quick! Bring the best robe and put it on him. Put a ring on his finger and sandals on his feet. Bring the fatted calf and kill it. Let's have a feast and celebrate. For this son of mine was dead and is alive again; he was lost and is found" (Luke 15:22-24).

That is the story Jesus told of the father's love, that is, of God's love. God loves us in Jesus Christ the way the prodigal's father loved his son. *God loves us without conditions.* "Will God be there for me?" we ask.

And the steadfast love of God that was present for us in Jesus Christ does not change. As the writer of the book of Hebrews puts it: "Jesus Christ is the same yesterday and today and forever" (Hebrews 13:8). What is that but another way of saying that God's steadfast love, God's unconditional love for sinful people, God's love for us in Jesus Christ, endures forever.

"Have I committed the unforgivable sin?" Chuck Knowlton asked anxiously from his prison cell. We know the anxiety of that question. "Will God be there for me?" we ask in our anxiety. The psalmist says yes. Our sins are forgiven. God's love endures forever.

"Will God forgive me?" Shawn Kerry asked her friend Michelle. We know the guilt that fills that question. "Will God be there for me?" we ask out of our own sense of guilt. The gospel says yes! "God so loved the world that he gave his one and only Son, that whoever believes in him shall not perish but have eternal life."

"Will God be there in my dying?" Anita Blocker asked. We know the fear that fills that question. "Will God be there for me in my dying?" we ask fearfully. The writer of the book of Hebrews says yes! "Jesus Christ is the same yesterday, today and forever."

Believe these promises of God. Focus your trust on the promises of God. Do not allow your focus to stay on yourself. Self-centered questions only lead us to despair. God's promises, on the other hand, lead us to life and hope. "God's love," after all, "endures forever."

8

How Can I Cope?

The Lord is my shepherd, I shall not be in want.
He makes me lie down in green pastures,
he leads me beside quiet waters,
he restores my soul.
He guides me in paths of righteousness for his name's sake.
Even though I walk through the valley of the shadow of
death,
I will fear no evil,
for you are with me;
Your rod and your staff,
they comfort me.
You prepare a table before me
in the presence of my enemies.
You anoint my head with oil;
my cup overflows.
Surely goodness and love will follow me
all the days of my life,
and I will dwell in the house of the Lord
forever.

Psalm 23

"I learned to see beyond the present," Clara told me. "I didn't see the wreck of a man my husband had become through alcoholism. I could see beyond him. I could still see the man that I married in spite of the scars, in spite of the years."

Clara, I soon learned, was a remarkable woman. Clara had learned how to cope. She had learned to cope with extreme adversity. In the latter years of her husband's life he lived in great pain. He often talked of suicide. Clara did not scold him for his thoughts. She let him be. She let him live his own life. She had the ability to remove herself from the situation, to step back from the pain and see things in a larger perspective.

Clara also accepted the fact that life constantly erects obstacles in our path. Clara knew that obstacles are a part of life whether we like them or not. Her obstacles did not make her unique. She was not the only person facing difficulty. She would live with the pain.

One day Clara had a dream. It was a terrifying dream. A huge black bear pursued her and sunk his claws into her flesh. She woke with a start. She was frightened. Soon she went back to sleep. Immediately, or so it seemed, she dreamed she was a butterfly living a transformed life.

Three days after her dream Clara came home from work at her usual time. There were some unusual signs around the house. The front porch light was not on. That was not like her husband. And the cat was in the house. That was not like her husband either. She went into her bedroom and looked around. There, on her bedstand, next to her clock, was her husband's watch and ring. She knew what had happened. He had gently prepared her for the real blow. She opened the door to his bedroom. Her husband lay dead with a self-inflicted bullet wound.

Clara called the police. When they came they found

her quite calm. "He wrote me the most beautiful note," she told them. The police were rather taken aback with her behavior. I was also taken aback when she told *me* her story. Never had I heard of anyone coping with such a tragedy in such a brave way.

"God prepared me for it," she told me. "That's what my dream was all about. That big bear was a symbol of my husband's death. But God transformed me through the pain. I became a butterfly. I had new life. Though I walked through the valley of the shadow of death, my Shepherd walked with me."

I am still touched by Clara's story. Clara is a marvelous woman of faith. She helps to teach me, she helps to teach all of us, how to cope with life's trials. There are at least three significant elements to her coping power. The first thing we can learn from Clara is *objectivity*. Clara lived in a very painful marriage, and yet, somehow, she could step back from her pain and see her situation in larger perspective. She could see beyond the present moment in her life. She could keep the present painful moment of life in perspective—in God's perspective. That is a marvelous mechanism for coping with difficult times.

A second thing that Clara teaches us is that we can cope with life a whole lot better when we realize that *life's difficulties touch us all*. That is the way life is. When we walk through fiery trials we ought to remember that we are not unique. We are not the only ones who have ever suffered. Suffering will weave its way into the tapestry of every life. We need to remember that. The rain will fall on every life. That fact does not remove the pain that touches us, but it helps us to cope. We expect some rainy days to cloud up our lives.

Finally, most importantly, Clara reminds us that the *Good Shepherd walks with us through life's trials*. Trials are not signs that God has abandoned us. How critical it is to remember that! There are many voices raised in American religious life today that seem to suggest that people who really believe in God will *not* suffer. God will keep the truly faithful from suffering. Suffering, therefore, is a clear sign of our lack of faith. But the Bible does not say that our Shepherd God will keep us from all trials. By no means! The Bible says that our Shepherd God will never forsake us. Our Shepherd God will walk with us through every time of trial, even through the valley of the shadow of death.

The Lord is our Shepherd! That is what Clara's story, that is what Clara's testimony, is all about. The Lord, our Shepherd, is with us. That is the presence we need in order to cope with the difficulties of life.

I once sat for several hours with a fine group of people. During the course of our time together we shared our personal stories. If you could have seen us, you would have concluded that we were a very ordinary group of people. Ordinary people we were, with extraordinary stories of pain to share. A pastor in the group shared the pain of raising his 16-year-old daughter. She was very independent. She walked her own rebellious way. Worst of all, perhaps, in a church that baptizes people upon profession of their faith, his daughter, the pastor's daughter, had refused to be baptized. He was left in pain. His daughter's rebellion left my clergyman friend in turmoil. He looked bewildered. He did not know how to cope with his family dilemma. He could only cling to the promise of the psalmist. He could only trust in the presence of the Shepherd God:

> The Lord is my shepherd, I shall not be in want;
>   he makes me lie down in green pastures.
> He leads me beside quiet waters,
>   he restores my soul.

He guides me in paths of righteousness
>   for his name's sake.
>> Psalm 23:1-3

A young woman in our group broke down and wept over her daughter's birth defect. There had been many operations and much money had been spent, but the problem and the pain lingered. This young woman grieved over the loss of what she expected motherhood to be. She wondered why this all happened to her. What had she done to deserve this? Would life ever turn out right? Her own childhood had been marred by a conflict-filled and abusive home. How much more pain would she have to suffer? Where would she find the energy to cope? She could cling to the promise of the psalmist. She could trust in the presence of the Shepherd God:

Even though I walk
>   through the valley of the shadow of death,
I will fear no evil,
>   for you are with me;
your rod and your staff,
>   they comfort me.
>> Psalm 23:4

Another woman in our group revealed some of the pain of her life. Her son had been killed in a swimming accident. She herself was a recovering alcoholic. Through the pain the family had endured, her husband had turned off his emotions. She was happy to be married to him, but there was not much spark of life between them. She hoped she could continue to manage her life and contain her grief. She hoped she could stay sober. She so wanted to be able to cope with life. She, too, could cling to the promise of the psalmist and trust in the presence of the Shepherd God:

You prepare a table before me
>   in the presence of my enemies.

You anoint my head with oil;
> my cup overflows.
Surely goodness and love will follow me
> all the days of my life,
and I will dwell in the house of the Lord
> forever.

Psalm 23:5-6

How can I cope? is a question we all ask at times. The challenge of coping with life is a universal human challenge. You would not have guessed by looking at the group of people I have spoken of that such serious problems lay just beneath the surface of life. If you are facing hardships, you are not alone in your struggles.

How shall I cope? What is the fear that lurks behind that question? For me I think it is the fear of failure. What if I fail myself and my Shepherd God? What if I fall into the abyss? What if I wander down a stray path? That will happen, you know. It will happen to you and it will happen to me. Such failures on our part, however, do not mean that God gives up on us.

One day Jesus told a parable about a sheep that had wandered from the path, a sheep that had lost its way.

"Suppose one of you has a hundred sheep and loses one of them. Does he not leave the ninety-nine in the open country and go after the lost sheep until he finds it? And when he finds it, he joyfully puts it on his shoulders."

Luke 15:4-5

The shepherd in Jesus' parable clearly acts towards the lost sheep the way our Shepherd God relates to us. This parable, therefore, is good news. Our Shepherd God will come to find us if we fail! Our Shepherd God will seek us out on our stray path. In fact, there is an entire choir of angels practicing to rejoice whenever God finds a lost sheep.

We may fail, at times, to cope with the problems that come cascading into our lives. Our failure to cope, however, does not doom us to a life lost from the watchful eye of God. Our Shepherd God has a special compassion for the lost! Our Shepherd God has a special compassion for you and for me, a compassion that never fails.

There is, after all, one great trial in life which not a single one of us can ultimately cope with—our death. No matter how well we cope with dying, we are all going to die. Death will defeat us. Death will snuff out our life. Jesus Christ, the Good Shepherd, has told us that he precedes us into the land of death.

"I am the good shepherd; I know my sheep and my sheep know me—just as the Father knows me and I know the Father—and I lay down my life for the sheep."
                                                            John 10:14-15

All the trials that we face in life are really anticipations of our final trial: death. The losses we experience anticipate this final loss. The griefs we endure anticipate death's final grief. We wonder whether we will be able to cope with life's trials. Sometimes we manage pretty well. Sometimes we fail. Our Shepherd Lord, however, never fails. Our Shepherd Lord has laid down his life that we might one day live in a land beyond all trials. So we walk through life and through death with the Good Shepherd, Jesus Christ, at our side. In Jesus' name we are bold to make the promise of the psalmist our own:

Even though I walk
    through the valley of the shadow of death,

I will fear no evil,
    for you are with me;
your rod and your staff,
    they comfort me.
            Psalm 23:4

9

Can God Heal Me?

Is any one of you in trouble? He should pray. Is any one happy? Let him sing songs of praise. Is any one of you sick? He should call the elders of the church to pray over him and anoint him with oil in the name of the Lord. And the prayer offered in faith will make the sick person well; the Lord will raise him up. If he has sinned, he will be forgiven. Therefore confess your sins to each other and pray for each other so that you may be healed. The prayer of a righteous man is powerful and effective. Elijah was a man just like us. He prayed earnestly that it would not rain. It did not rain on the land for three and a half years. Again he prayed, and the heavens gave rain, and the earth produced its crops.

James 5:13-18

Right away I recognized his voice on the phone. It was Ken Lyons. He sounded a bit hoarse. "Pastor Jensen," he said, "I haven't been feeling very well lately. I've been to a couple of doctors and they don't seem to know what to think. Each of them had a prescription for me but it hasn't worked. If anything, I'm feeling worse."

"What can I do for you, Ken?" I asked.

"I don't know exactly, pastor. Well, remember at our prayer group the other night? You talked about healing as being God's will for our lives. Can God heal me, Pastor Jensen? Would you be willing to have a healing service for me? I think I need your prayers."

"Sure, we can have a healing service," I agreed. "What about Wednesday evening?" Wednesday was fine with Ken, so I planned the healing service. I called a couple of Ken's friends in the congregation and asked them if they would be willing to attend the service at Ken's home. They agreed.

About eight of us gathered at Ken Lyon's place on Wednesday evening. I asked Ken to share his medical problem with the group. Once everyone knew the nature of Ken's illness, I explained what we were going to do. We were going to have a service of Holy Communion together. Before the sharing of the bread and wine, I invited them to pray for Ken, laying their hands upon his head. "Pray that he be healed," I instructed them. "Don't pray that God's will be done for Ken as if we don't know God's will," I said. *"God's will is our healing!* So pray boldly, claiming God's healing presence for Ken. Following your prayers, we will share the body and blood of Christ. *God is the one who does the healing here.* Healing doesn't come through our prayers or through our faith. Healing comes from God. What better way to invite God's healing presence than to take the body and blood of God's Son into our bodies?"

We had our service. Each person present laid his or her hands on Ken and boldly prayed for healing. As a small community of Christian people, we shared the bread and the wine. It was a very meaningful and moving time that we spent together. Many tears were shed. Our hopes were high.

Early the next morning my telephone rang. It was Ken.

He'd had a strange experience in the night. "I woke up," he said to me, "with this warmth flowing through my body. I didn't know what to think. I couldn't go back to sleep so I got up and stood at my living room window staring out at the beautiful night sky. As I stood there, warmed through and through, it became clear to me that this was the hand of God."

Ken was right. His symptoms cleared up almost immediately. His doctors were surprised, but pronounced him well. In, with, and under the bread and wine, God had poured healing power into Ken Lyons' body. This event took place quite early in my ministry. I will never forget it.

"Can God heal me?" Ken had asked. The answer to Ken's question is clearly *yes*. Yes, God can heal you. It is to state the obvious to say that Ken Lyons is not the only person who ever got sick and wondered about God's healing presence. I have wondered about that myself. Many of you reading this have wondered as well. Can God heal me? That is a common human question.

There is no doubt that the healing of diseased bodies was a central reality in Jesus' ministry. In Matthew 9:35, for example, we read:

Jesus went through all the towns and villages, teaching in their synagogues, preaching the good news of the kingdom and healing every disease and sickness.

Reading through the Gospels, we come across story after story in which Jesus transforms sickness into health. Jesus brought salvation to people. Jesus came among people as the Savior. *His salvation was that human life be all that it was intended to be in God's creative plan. Jesus, therefore, pushed back all of the forces that stood against the fullness of human life.* Where sin was an obstacle to the fullness of life,

Jesus spoke a word of forgiveness. Where evil powers were an obstacle to the fullness of life, Jesus drove out the demons. Where sickness was an obstacle to fullness of life, Jesus brought health. Finally, because death was the last enemy of life, Jesus rose from the grave with an offer of eternal life to all believers. "I have come that [you] may have life, and have it to the full," Jesus said (John 10:10b).

There is simply no way around the reality that *restoring diseased bodies to health was a central and integral part of Jesus' earthly ministry.* Healing of bodies was an indispensable part of Jesus' offer of salvation. We would have to omit large chunks of the Gospels if we want to talk about Jesus' life and ministry and not talk about healing.

Yet I know people do just that. Probably the most common way to get around the relevance of Jesus' healing ministry is to treat that ministry as a kind of side show. In other words, Jesus' healing miracles were just for effect. They show us that Jesus really is the Son of God. Other than that, they are of no benefit to us. I read and hear claims like that all the time. But I do not believe such claims. Jesus' ministry of healing was not a side show. Jesus' healing ministry is an integral part of his offer of salvation—even in the 20th century.

The Scripture which is the basis of this chapter is from the book of James. It is clear from the passage that prayers for healing were a normal part of the life and practice of the early church. "Is anyone of you sick?" the author asks. "He [or she] should call the elders of the church to pray over him and anoint him with oil in the name of the Lord. And the prayer offered in faith will make the sick person well; the Lord will raise him up . . ." (James 5:14-15a). It is instructive to me that James calls for the elders, for the representatives of the community or congregation, to gather for the prayers of healing. Prayers for healing are not normally conducted simply between the one who prays and the one who is sick. That kind of prayer in isolation from the Christian community might suggest a kind of magic. *Prayers for healing, rather, should normally take place within a gathered community of God's people.* That was one of the reasons I invited members of the congregation to be part of the healing for Ken Lyons.

When possible, the Sunday morning service is an ideal occasion for prayers of healing. Prayers for healing in a service where Holy Communion is served are particularly fitting. It is then clear to everyone present that the focus of God's healing presence is through bread and wine and not through the particular power of those who have prayed for the sick. God is the healer, after all!

James says two other words here that we need to heed. He says, first of all, that *the prayer offered in faith will heal the sick person.* This is a call to bold praying. When we pray for the sick we ought to pray in faith. We ought to pray believing that God really wants to heal us. Healing, after all, is God's will for us. We sometimes hear people refer to a disease of the body as God's will. "It must be God's will that I got cancer," someone might say. I do not believe that! Disease is a part of our fallen and sinful and broken world. It is true that God can work all things together for good. (See Romans 8:28.) God can bring good out of our fallen condition. But God did not will for us to live in a broken world!

Prayers of faith for the sick are important, James tells us. Now it is true that some people seem to have a gift of healing prayer. According to the apostle Paul, *the gift of healing is one of the gifts of the Spirit* (see 1 Corinthians 12:9). Such people are truly a gift to us from God. But let us be careful here. Such persons have been given a gift of God.

It is not that they have more faith than the rest of us. It is not that they pray more effectively than the rest of us. Neither of these is the case. The reality is that the Spirit has chosen to gift them in this particular way just as the Spirit gifts us in other ways. Those among us with gifts of healing are God's gift to us.

The great danger in talk about healing lies very close at hand in this conversation. "The prayer offered in faith will make the sick person well," James says. *The danger is that we might hear this to mean that people are healed because of the faith of the one who prays.* We might call this "faith healing." The formula that is sometimes put forth here is that healing will happen if we pray in true faith. If healing does not happen, that is a sign that our prayers and our faith are not *true* prayers of faith. That kind of formula is guaranteed to produce false guilt within us. It means that all our unanswered prayers for healing are our fault. We believe and pray but no healing takes place. That is our fault. Our faith is not true. Our prayers are somehow inadequate. This understanding of "faith healing" is bound to cause great difficulty.

I do not think there is such a thing as "faith healing." That is the second word from James that we need to hear. "The Lord will raise him up." That is what James says. Certainly we are to pray in bold faith believing that God's healing can happen. *But it is not our faith that brings the healing into being.* God brings the healing. *God is the healer.* God holds the power of healing in God's hand. Our prayers and our faith do not heal people. God heals people!

But if that is so, and if healing is clearly God's will for us in Jesus Christ, why is it that so often our prayers for healing are not answered? I am going to be quite bold at this point and say our faithful prayers for healing are always answered. God's will is to heal. "Can God heal me?" we ask. The answer is *yes! God not only can but God will heal our bodies from all disease in the day of the great resurrection.* Resurrection day is God's final day of healing for all of us!

God's resurrection power, God's healing power, sometimes breaks into our lives on this side of the resurrection. Some of us experience healing already in this life. That was true for my friend Ken Lyons. For this we can only praise God. But why him and not you or not me? I do not know. The answer to that question is known to God alone. We never know when the healing power of the resurrection that is to come might break in on our bodies already here in this world. We pray that it might be so!

"Can God heal me?" we ask. The answer is *yes.* God's will is that we be whole again. God will bring that wholeness and healing to pass for all believers in the day of resurrection. In some of our lives God will also gracefully break in with God's healing power on this side of the great resurrection.

God in heaven, for Jesus' sake send your Holy Spirit upon us; drive away all sickness of body and spirit; make whole that which is broken; deliver us from the power of the devil; and preserve us in true faith to share in the power of Christ's resurrection and to serve you with all the saints now and evermore. Amen.

10

How Shall We Live in a Nuclear World?

This is the word that came to Jeremiah from the LORD in the tenth year of Zedekiah king of Judah, which was the eighteenth year of Nebuchadnezzar. The army of the king of Babylon was then besieging Jerusalem, and Jeremiah the prophet was confined in the courtyard of the guard in the royal palace of Judah. . . .

Jeremiah said, "The word of the LORD came to me: Hanamel son of Shallum your uncle is going to come to you and say, 'Buy my field at Anathoth, because as nearest relative it is your right and duty to buy it.'

"Then, just as the LORD had said, my cousin Hanamel came to me in the courtyard of the guard and said, 'Buy my field at Anathoth in the territory of Benjamin. Since it is your right to redeem it and possess it, buy it for yourself.'

"I knew that this was the word of the LORD; so I bought the field at Anathoth from my cousin Hanamel and weighed out for him seventeen shekels of silver. I signed and

sealed the deed, had it witnessed, and weighed out the silver on the scales. I took the deed of purchase—the sealed copy containing the terms and conditions, as well as the unsealed copy—and I gave this deed to Baruch son of Neriah, the son of Mahseiah, in the presence of my cousin Hanamel and of the witnesses who had signed the deed and of all the Jews sitting in the courtyard of the guard.

"In their presence I gave Baruch these instructions: 'This is what the LORD Almighty, the God of Israel, says: Take these documents, both the sealed and unsealed copies of the deed of purchase, and put them in a clay jar so they will last a long time. For this is what the LORD Almighty, the God of Israel, says: Houses, fields and vineyards will again be bought in this land.'

Jeremiah 32:1-2, 6-15

"Happy birthday, Grandpa," the young boy said. "I'm glad you're 60 years old. I wish I could get to be 60 some day."

"What do you mean?" the grandfather replied. "Why can't you be 60 some day?"

"Because the bombs will get me first," the grandchild said with fear in his eyes.

This was an actual conversation. Those kinds of conversations take place in today's world, in today's nuclear world. In his book, *The Fate of the Earth*, Jonathan Schell eloquently states the reality that we all know is out there:

The spectre of extinction hovers over our world and shapes our lives with its invisible but terrible pressure. It now accompanies us through life, from birth to death. Wherever we go, it goes, too; in whatever we do, it is present. It gets up with us in the morning, it stays at our side throughout the day, and it gets into bed with us at night. It is with us in the delivery room, at the marriage ceremony, and on our deathbeds. It is the truth about the way we now live. But such a life cannot go on for long (New York: Alfred A. Knopf, Inc. 1982).

"Such a life cannot go on for long." That is what we all know and fear, isn't it? Someone might lose patience; someone might push the button; someone might panic. How do we live in such a world? How do we live in a world loaded with nuclear explosives?

That is not an idle question. It is a real and terrible fear as opposed to an anxiety attack. Anxiety is never attached to a specific cause. Fear has a cause. People who are afraid can point to the cause. People who fear the nuclear night point to the cause of their fear. One way they do that is by citing the statistics. For example, they point to the fact that one Poseidon submarine has the equivalent of three times the firepower used in World War II. In other words, if you added up all the explosives that were used in World War II, it would be only one-third the explosive power carried by one Poseidon submarine. And we have 31 of these submarines! The new Trident submarine is even more powerful. It has the equivalent of eight times the firepower used in World War II. That is enough power to destroy every major city in the northern hemisphere. And that is only half the explosive power out there. The Soviet Union has the other half. When you think about the destructive power that is now at our fingertips, and realize that human beings tend to use the weapons of destruction they invent, there is certainly cause for fear. How do we live in a nuclear world?

One of the ways we have chosen to live in such a world is to *deny* that there really is a serious problem. That is what human beings always do with the topic of death. Ernest Becker wrote a Pulitzer prize-winning book in 1973 entitled,

The Denial of Death. His thesis is that one of the fundamental motifs of all human behavior is our zeal to deny the reality of death. Clearly, our desire to deny death's reality has to work overtime in order to deny the incredible forces that can bring death to today's world. But we do it.

It has been discovered by counselors, for example, that though both parents and children know explosive powers abound and life is threatened, the subject hardly ever comes up in home conversations. Someone said *the realistic fear of nuclear war is the new family secret.* No one talks about it. We pretend it is not there.

This is one of the reasons Jonathan Schell wrote his book, *The Fate of the Earth.* He refers to the failure of response. Millions of people know the nuclear threat to life exists, but hardly anyone does anything about it. We go on, he observes, living as if all is well with the world. "But this feeling of well-being is based on a *denial* of the most important reality of our time, and therefore is itself a kind of sickness" (Schell, p. 8).

We cannot live in a nuclear world with our stereo headsets blaring in our ears and drowning out the cries of warning. We cannot deny the danger that exists. We cannot wish it out of existence. Keeping it a "family secret" will not do. The first thing we are called upon to do is to *face the reality of the situation.*

Some Christians have said that God would not allow a nuclear nightmare to take place. They find that a cause for comfort. It is also a cause for inactivity. We do not need to worry about it and we do not need to do anything about it because God will take care of it. I do not believe that. I think human beings just might bring down the end of history upon ourselves. I find nothing in the Bible to tell me that cannot happen. If we are capable of bringing forth the destruction, then we as Christians have a responsibility to work for peace as an alternative to war. Facing the reality of the situation, *Christian people are called to work for peace;* we are called to work that God's kingdom may come on earth as it is in heaven.

There is a second reality about this world-threatening situation. Our world is threatened, but the situation is not hopeless. Christian people remain a people of hope. God will have the last word. God has had the last word in Jesus Christ. Jesus Christ has defeated our last enemy. Jesus Christ has destroyed death's power over us. God raised Jesus from the dead. *Death,* therefore, *holds no power over us.* Should the nuclear genie be let out of its bottle, that is not going to derail God's creation of a new heaven and a new earth. Devastating as it is, nuclear destruction would not be the last word to be spoken over life in this universe. The God of this universe will not let it be so. God's life is stronger than death. The last word to be spoken, the last act to take place with our world, is "the resurrection of the body and the life everlasting." That is one Christian confession of faith. "We believe in the resurrection of the body and life everlasting." Thus believing, *we are people of hope*—we are people of hope in a nuclear world.

Paul the apostle sets forth the courage of our hope in a powerful passage from Romans 8. Paul writes:

No, in all these things we are more than conquerors through the one who loved us. For I am sure that neither death, nor life, nor angels, nor principalities, nor things present, nor things to come, nor powers, nor height, nor depth, nor anything else in all creation, will be able to separate us from the love of God in Christ Jesus our Lord.

Romans 8:37-39 (LCP)

We look and we see nations preparing to conquer each

other. *We believe* that we are more than conquerors through him who loved us.

We look and we see tremendous amounts of destructive power being stockpiled on this earth. *We believe* that neither death, nor life, nor angels, nor principalities will be able to separate us from the love of God in Christ Jesus our Lord.

We look and we see explosive power encircling the earth with plans on the military drawing boards for ever more sophisticated weapons. *We believe* that neither things present nor things to come nor powers will be able to separate us from the love of God in Christ Jesus our Lord.

We look and we see missiles in the depths of the sea and in the depths of the earth that are ready to be launched through the heavens for our destruction. *We believe* that neither height, nor depth, nor anything else in all creation will be able to separate us from the love of God in Christ Jesus our Lord.

We are, in other words, a people of hope. As people of hope, we are able to do what many people in our world cannot do. *We are able to commit acts of hope.* That is what Jeremiah did in his day. The world as he knew it was under siege. Mighty Babylon was on the brink of crushing tiny Jerusalem. Jeremiah followed the events from his prison cell. His personal situation could not have looked more hopeless.

Then, in the midst of this hopeless situation, Jeremiah's cousin came and asked Jeremiah to buy his field at Anathoth. Think about that for a minute! It is a ridiculous scene. Just as Babylon is about to conquer the whole land, Jeremiah is asked to buy a field. But Jeremiah did it! He bought the field because he believed the promise of God that said: "Houses and fields and vineyards shall again be bought in this land" (Jeremiah 32:15). Jeremiah believed in the promises of God. Jeremiah was a person of hope. As a person of hope, he committed—what to most people must have seemed insane—an act of hope.

Jeremiah's wild and crazy act of hope reminds me of something Luther once said. He was asked what he would do if he knew the world would end tomorrow. Luther replied: "I'd plant a tree." As a people of hope, we today are called to walk in the footsteps of Jeremiah and Luther. We are called to commit acts of hope.

Let me suggest for you some specific acts of hope we can commit in our nuclear-threatened world. We can buy fields. We can plant apple trees or gardens or whatever we love to plant. We can inform ourselves and vote for those candidates we think will best work for peace. We can write to our elected officials urging them to think peace. We can renounce force and violence as a means of solving problems in our own lives. We can pray for peace. We can have a peace emphasis Sunday in our congregation. We can relate to or visit churches in the land of our enemy in order to create good will and better understanding. We can attend a peace workshop. We can read a book on peace issues.

The list can go on and on. You can add to it any way you wish. The important thing is that we realize that we are people of hope. We are people of hope because of what God in Jesus Christ has done to death. We are people of hope because we believe in the resurrection of the body and the life everlasting. As people of hope, we are called to commit acts of hope. That is how we choose to live in a nuclear world.